W9-BYY-075

Sisters

by Lola M. Schaefer

Consulting Editor: Gail Saunders-Smith, Ph.D.

Consultant: Phyllis Edelbrock, First-Grade Teacher,
University Place School District, Washington

Pebble Books

an imprint of Capstone Press
Mankato, Minnesota

Pebble Books are published by Capstone Press
818 North Willow Street, Mankato, Minnesota 56001
http://www.capstone-press.com

Library of Congress Cataloging-in-Publication Data
Schaefer, Lola M., 1950–
    Sisters/by Lola M. Schaefer.
    p. cm.—(Families)
    Includes bibliographical references and index.
    Summary: Photographs and simple text describe sisters and some of the
activities they do together.
    ISBN 0-7368-0260-6
    1. Sisters—Juvenile literature. [1. Sisters.] I. Title. II. Series: Schaefer, Lola M.,
1950–   Families.
HQ759.96.S33   1999
306.875′4—dc21
                                                              98-46135
                                                                  CIP
                                                                   AC

Note to Parents and Teachers

The Families series supports national social studies standards for
units related to identifying family members and their roles in the
family. This book describes and illustrates sisters and activities they
do together. The photographs support emergent readers in
understanding the text. The repetition of words and phrases
helps emergent readers learn new words. This book also introduces
emergent readers to subject-specific vocabulary words, which are
defined in the Words to Know section. Emergent readers may need
assistance to read some words and to use the Table of Contents,
Words to Know, Read More, Internet Sites, and Index/Word List
sections of the book.

Table of Contents

Sisters 5

Sisters Play Inside 9

Sisters Play Outside. 15

Note to Parents and Teachers . . . 2

Words to Know 22

Read More 23

Internet Sites. 23

Index/Word List. 24

Sisters can have brothers.

Sisters can have sisters.

Sisters dress up.

Sisters play games.

12

Sisters teach.

Sisters eat watermelon.

Sisters hang upside down.

Sisters build snowmen.

Sisters smile.

Words to Know

brother—a boy or man who has the same parents as another person

dress up—to put on fancy clothing or adult clothing and pretend to be someone else

sister—a girl or woman who has the same parents as another person

snowman—a figure built with snow; people build snowmen by stacking large balls of snow.

teach—to show someone how to do something

watermelon—a large juicy fruit that grows on vines; watermelon usually has a thick, green rind, many seeds, and watery pulp.

Read More

Bailey, Debbie. *Sisters.* North York, Ont., Canada: Annick Press, 1993.

Gans, Lydia. *Sisters, Brothers, and Disability: A Family Album.* Minneapolis: Fairview Press, 1997.

Rosenberg, Maxine B. *Mommy's in the Hospital Having a Baby.* New York: Clarion Books, 1997.

Saunders-Smith, Gail. *Families.* People. Mankato, Minn.: Pebble Books, 1997.

Internet Sites

The Family Fun Network—Kids Room
http://www.ffn.org/kids.htm

Girl Tech
http://www.girltech.com

Just 4 Kids
http://www.herald.ns.ca/news/kids.html

Index/Word List

brothers, 5
build, 19
dress up, 9
eat, 15
games, 11
hang, 17
play, 11

sisters, 5, 7, 9, 11, 13, 15, 17, 19, 21
smile, 21
snowmen, 19
teach, 13
upside down, 17
watermelon, 15

Word Count: 28
Early-Intervention Level: 5

Editorial Credits
Mari C. Schuh, editor; Steve Weil/Tandem Design, cover designer and illustrator; Kimberly Danger and Sheri Gosewisch, photo researchers

Photo Credits
Cheryl A. Ertelt, 4
International Stock/Michael Paras, cover
Kay L. Hendrich, 16
Oscar C. Williams, 6
PhotoBank, Inc./M. Diamond, 20
Photo Network/Tom McCarthy, 10
Rainbow/Linda K. Moore, 14
Shaffer Photography/James L. Shaffer, 1
Transparencies, Inc./Tom and Dee Ann McCarthy, 8; Tom McCarthy, 12
Visuals Unlimited/D. Cavagnah, 18

Special thanks to Joy Allison, Lori Hollenback, and Penny McCarthy, first-grade teachers at Evergreen Primary in University Place, Washington, for reviewing books in the Families series.